Together Time

SPIRIT WITH US

Activities With Ages 11 to 14

Judith Dunlap and
Mary Cummins Wlodarski

ST. ANTHONY MESSENGER PRESS
Cincinnati, Ohio

Nihil Obstat: Rev. Nicholas Lohkamp, O.F.M.
Rev. Edward J. Gratsch

Imprimi Potest: Rev. John Bok, O.F.M.

Imprimatur: Archdiocese of Cincinnati
July 22, 1997

Cover and front matter illustrations by Steve Erspamer, S.M.
Cover and book design by Sanger & Eby Design

ISBN 0-86716-292-9

Published by St. Anthony Messenger Press
Printed in the U.S.A.

Contents

INTRODUCTION

Dear parent, grandparent, guardian, godparent, sponsor or other caring adult,

An old saying is profoundly true: "Faith is caught, not taught." And faith is caught from those people who are closest to us. This book, *Together Time*, offers you a simple and fun opportunity to play "catch" with the special young person or persons in your life. The activities and discussion questions are based on everyday experiences. They offer simple and practical ways of engaging a youngster in faith-talk.

We realize that faith-talk is not easy for many of us grown-up Catholics. But we also know that if God and prayer, faith, hope and Christian charity are going to be a reality in the lives of our children, they will have to hear grown-ups talk about God and hear them pray, and witness their acts of charity. We hope that *Together Time* offers an easy, not too time-consuming way of accomplishing this.

The time you spend together in each session is not lesson time. It is a sharing time. It is an opportunity for you to share one of the most precious gifts God has given you—your faith. It is a gift that our young people have also been blessed with. They need your help, however, to discover some of its many facets and to make it a conscious part of their lives.

We ask you to take the risk of sharing yourself and your faith with the special young persons in your life. Take the time, and we promise that as the years go by you will not regret it. In the process of helping your youngster "catch" the faith, you will discover how often you find yourself on the receiving end.

Enjoy your time together. It is another gift from God. In your "together time" and in your alone time, may you be aware of God's constant presence in your life.

Through, with and in Jesus,

Judith Dunlap

Mary Cummins Wlodarski

How to use this book:

Together Time sessions usually take about forty-five minutes. The time you spend together may actually be shorter or longer, depending on how long your discussion takes.

It is helpful to meet as regularly as possible. Meeting at the same time on the same day of the week will help keep you on track. It is also helpful to meet in the same place.

Before You Meet, prepare for the session by following the suggestions offered. Look over the Activity and gather any supplies (papers, pencils, crayons and so on) you may need. If possible, read over the Grown-up's Page and the Story before you sit down with your child. (Most sessions include one or more Activity Pages for the youngster to complete alone. While a child solves the puzzle or finds the way through the maze, you will have time to review the Grown-up's Page.)

Set the Environment. Try to make the place where you meet special so that the youngster knows that this is a special time. Simple steps (such as lighting a candle, setting out a Bible, using a small cloth or table covering) can turn any table into a prayerful space. Ask the youngster to help set up the space.

The **Theme** statement encapsulates the point of the session. A brief explanation refines and clarifies it for you.

Getting Started (ten minutes): These questions help introduce the Story's theme by asking people to look at their own life experiences.

Read the Story (ten minutes): Older youngsters can read the material alone. Read the material aloud if you wish.

Discuss the Story (ten minutes): The questions offered are only meant to get you started. You may certainly add any other questions you think apply. It is also possible that a story may trigger a very different insight in you or the child. Respect yourself and your child enough to discuss the subject openly.

The Activities (ten minutes) are meant to give adults and young people some time to work on separate but parallel projects. Sometimes the activity may ask you to work together. (You will also find suggestions for preschoolers to work on at the same time.) Before beginning your own activity, go over the directions for the child's activity page. When the youngster is clear about what to do, you may both begin working.

The Closing Rituals (five minutes) are times for prayer together. As such, they are essential to the program. The subject matter of this series is our relationship to God. Study alone cannot form faith, any more than reading about someone makes that person your friend.

Do not feel limited by these suggestions. As you and your young person begin to share, you may discover types of prayer and rituals that are more meaningful and more comfortable. How you pray together is not as important as taking the time to pray together.

Use the same ritual gesture in each Prayer Time. Make a small cross with your thumb on your forehead, lips and heart as you say, "Lord, we ask you to open our minds, our lips and our hearts to the Good News in your gospel, so that we may live it in the days ahead."

THE SPIRIT AT WORK

Before You Meet

Read the material below. Read "The Spirit at Work" in *Spirit With Us*.

The Third Person of the Holy Trinity, the Holy Spirit, may be a difficult concept for young persons. The Spirit was left with us by Jesus so we would continue to be aware that God loves us and has a Plan, the Reign of God, for how we should live. We are called to love God, to love ourselves and to love others. As the doxology in our Sunday Mass reminds us, we live *through, with* and *in* Jesus, and in the unity of the Holy Spirit. This is what enables us to be true followers of Christ.

Theme. The Reign of God happens whenever we live with love for God.

There are three persons—Father, Son and Spirit—in our one God. This is the teaching we call the Holy Trinity. Just as we live in relationships, so God lives in relationship both within God and with us. This is a central belief and a deep mystery, something we know through God's revelation but do not completely understand. God creates us, redeems us and saves us. These three actions show us God's love and grace.

Optional Activity. Go through the pictures in a children's Bible, Bible storybooks or other such books to find pictures of Jesus and God. Ask your young person to draw God however he or she best imagines God to be. These drawings may be symbolic rather than portraits of God.

Together Time

Set the Environment. With the help of your young person, prepare your meeting space. Open with a prayer.

Getting Started. Who are some of the people you love? How do you show your love? How do they show their love to you?

Read the Story. Ask your young person to retell the story to you.

The following questions may encourage discussion.

1) What do we mean when we talk about the Plan or Reign of God?

2) Who are the three Persons in the Holy Trinity? How do we see the actions of these three Persons today?

3) Read through the titles of each section of the children's book. What do you think these titles say about how the Spirit is with us?

Activity. On the next page is an activity to be completed together.

Closing Ritual. Come together and share your stories of how God is with you. Then pray together the petitions you wrote for the Spirit of God. Finish by praying together the doxology: "Through Jesus, in Jesus, and with Jesus, in the unity of the Holy Spirit, all glory and honor be yours, Almighty Father, forever and ever. Amen."

My Story of God's Spirit

Think about what in your life brought you to this day and this time.

Are there times when God was obviously present to you through community? With forgiveness and action? In prayer? Then there are the times when you are aware of the Spirit at work?

Write one of your stories in the flame below. Ask your young person to write his or her story in the space around the flame.

Petitions to the Spirit

Finish the sentences below together.

Spirit of God, we know you work through us when we _______________________.

Spirit of God, we know you are present with us when we _______________________.

Spirit of God, we know you are alive in our world when we _______________________.

PENTECOST: THE DAY THE SPIRIT CAME

Before You Meet

Read the materials below. Read "Pentecost: The Day the Spirit Came" in *Spirit With Us*.

This retelling of the event of Pentecost comes from the first two chapters of the Acts of the Apostles. Pentecost is often called "the birthday of the Church" because receiving the Spirit enabled the apostles to preach and build community. God wants us to continue being a Church family. The Church helps us grow ever closer to God and to each other through the sacraments.

Theme. The Spirit of God is with us. Great things happen when we are open to the Spirit.

Peter promised those who listened to him at the first Pentecost that great things would happen. This promise is with us today! Peter used Old Testament stories and the stories of Jesus' life to convince those around him that the Messiah had come. We are saved by Jesus our Messiah, and we are called to do great things. Our present lives continue to teach us this, whatever our age.

Optional Activity. Look at family pictures of weddings, Baptisms, First Communions or Confirmations. Notice how special we make these moments with fancy clothes, flowers, rings and so on. Make note also about who we invite to be with us at such cherished events.

Together Time

Set the Environment. Open with a prayer, perhaps "Come, Holy Spirit."

Getting Started. What makes a special event "special" for you? What everyday events do you make special? How?

Read the Story. The following questions may encourage discussion:

1) What was your favorite part of the story? Why?

2) How did Jesus' friends feel after Jesus ascended into heaven? How did that change?

3) Pretend you were in the crowd listening to the disciples and Peter at Pentecost. What would you have thought? What would you have done?

Activity. On the next page is an activity for you to start separately and complete together.

Closing Ritual. Sit together with your weaving. Thank God by naming all the people in your stories and in the weaving. Finish with, "Through Jesus, with Jesus, and in Jesus, in the unity of the Holy Spirit, all glory and honor is yours, Almighty Father, forever and ever. Amen."

The Spirit Weaves With Our Lives

Our stories, woven in with the stories of the Bible and with the sacraments, form the fabric of salvation.

Using the stories in and around the flame (the previous Together Page), write a title for your story on the strip below. (Your young person's Together Page also has a strip.) When all are finished, cut on the dotted lines and feed your strips into the weaving below.

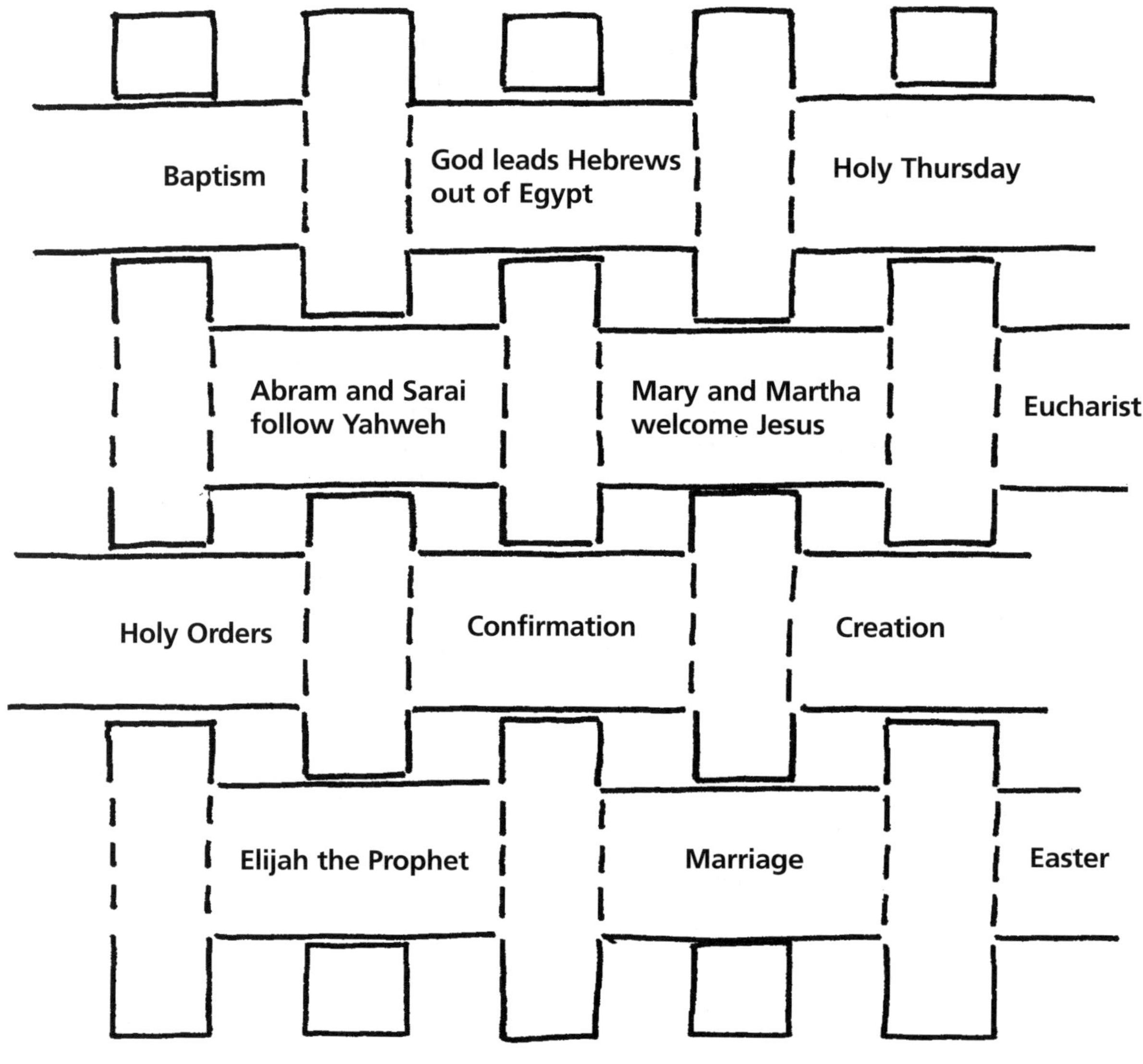

Your strip:

Speaking in Tongues

At Pentecost, the disciples amazed everyone by speaking in many different languages. Each listener could understand what was being said.

Below are some words that come from the Pentecost story. Can you unscramble them to make sense?

SLEPASOT _ _ _ _ _ _ _ _

YHLO TIPSIR _ _ _ _ _ _ _ _ _ _

GIREN FO ODG _ _ _ _ _ _ _ _ _ _

CEPSENTOT _ _ _ _ _ _ _ _ _

TALSAONIV _ _ _ _ _ _ _ _ _

SONCINEAS _ _ _ _ _ _ _ _ _

PLICESSID _ _ _ _ _ _ _ _ _

REPTE _ _ _ _ _

RYAM _ _ _ _

The Spirit Weaves Our Lives Together

You wrote a story about how God and the Spirit have already acted in your life in our first activity. Think about that story again. This activity is going to ask you to look even deeper into that story. This is called "reflection," and it is a way for us to stop and identify when God is with us.

In your story:

How old were you?

Who was with you?

Where did you live at that time?

What school did you attend?

Who was your best friend?

How did you feel at the time this happened?

How did it turn out?

On the Together Page is a weaving. Please title your story reflection and write that title on the strip below. Then cut out the strip and weave it into "the fabric of salvation." (You may make more strips if you like.)

Your strip:

SPIRIT OF BELONGING

Before You Meet

Read the materials below. Read "Spirit of Belonging" in *Spirit With Us*.

    We all need to belong to someone or something to feel connected and not alone. First and foremost, we all belong to God. This section of stories deals with the desire we all have to be part of God's family. The Catholic Church recognizes this desire, and receives new members through the Sacrament of Baptism.

Theme. The Sacrament of Baptism gives us new life and makes us members of our Church family, the Catholic community.

    Once we feel welcome someplace, we are free to be our true selves. Acceptance provides us with the strength to act in kindness and with justice. Belonging isn't simply a "warm feeling"; it is the foundation upon which we build our lives.

Optional Activity. List groups you have belonged to in the past or still belong to. Have your young person do the same. What have each of these groups done for you? Also watch television shows to see how groups form and how people relate to each other as family or friends.

Together Time

Set the Environment. Open with a prayer.

Getting Started. When was the last time you felt truly accepted or appreciated? What happened as a result?

Read the Story. The following questions may encourage discussion.

1) When are you most likely to feel lonely? Why?

2) When are you most likely to feel accepted and/or wanted? Why?

3) How can you show others in your life that you welcome them?

Activity. On the reverse is an activity for you to do together.

Closing Ritual. Water is the main symbol of Baptism. Place a pitcher of water and an empty bowl on your table. Pour the water into the bowl, saying, "Spirit of God, wash me in love." When the bowl is full, use the water to bless yourselves and each other with the Sign of the Cross. Close with the doxology: "Through Jesus, in Jesus, and with Jesus, in the unity of the Holy Spirit, all glory and honor is yours, Almighty Father, forever and ever. Amen."

Within a Circle of Friends

What are some words that describe how you feel when you know you belong?
What are some ways you can help others feel like they belong?
Write these words on the T-shirts of the people in the drawing below.

The Baptism Ceremony

Fill in the missing words:

"I baptize you in the name of the _ _ _ _ _ _ _, and of the _ _ _, and of the

_ _ _ _ _ _ _ _ _ _ _. A _ _ _."

PHILIP AND THE ETHIOPIAN

Before You Meet

Read the materials below. Read "Philip and the Ethiopian" in *Spirit With Us*.

The first Christians were Jews. They were awaiting the Messiah, and it was the Hebrew Scriptures that the disciples used in their preaching. But Jesus' message soon reached outside the Jewish community. Disciples like Philip traveled to many lands. This story tells of a time when that message went all the way to Ethiopia, where a vibrant Christian community developed. The story can be found in Acts 8:4-40.

Theme. We need to risk talking about God so we and others can grow in faith and love.

We learn about God in many ways, but certainly the most common way is by listening. We listen to parents, teachers, clergy and other committed Christians. After we learn about Jesus, then we have another responsibility: We have to speak to others and share our faith! Talking about God is what disciples do.

Optional Activity. Prepare a small notebook by writing on it "What we know about God." Then use it as a scrapbook, a place to save pictures, articles, stories, jokes—whatever. Add to your memories of God anytime you recognize them.

Together Time

Set the Environment. Open with a prayer.

Getting Started. Who was the first person to tell you about God? Or who was your favorite teacher? Why?

Read the Story. The following questions may encourage discussion.

1) What was your favorite part of the story? Why?

2) Do you feel more like Philip or more like the Ethiopian? Why?

3) Who talks to you about God? To whom do you talk about God? What are you saying?

Activity. On the next page is an activity for you to do separately and then bring together. Let younger children color the church.

Closing Ritual. Read together the very same passage from the prophet Isaiah that the Ethiopian was reading, Isaiah 43:1-7. What promise do you hear in this reading? End with the Our Father.

Building a Church of Belonging and Welcome

We are greeted and welcomed many times at church on Sunday by particular people, at certain times in the Mass, with phrases you hear. All these help build up our church family.

Name five things that happen at your church to make you feel welcome.

1)____

2)____

3)____

4)____

5)____

When your children have finished their reflections, come up with a common list of five things that make you feel welcome. After all, the more we feel that we belong, the more real the Church becomes to us.

As you make your list, the youngest child can color the church building.

1)______________________________

2)______________________________

3)______________________________

4)______________________________

5)______________________________

Searching for the Right Words

The Ethiopian was reading Scripture, but he wanted to understand even more. He was willing to search for meaning, and Philip was very happy to oblige!

How good are your "searching" skills? Can you find the words in the puzzle below?

Look for:

- BELIEVE
- PHILIP
- ETHIOPIA
- AFRICA
- BAPTISM
- SCRIPTURE
- ANGEL
- WATER
- CHARIOT
- ROAD

```
R O A D O R E T A W
K R C S T I V J S A
B M I E S E P H C I
E L R L P T I P R P
L E F T P H I L I P
I B A P T I S M P E
L R R O G O E R T J
V A C O B P N I U C
E C H A R I O T R H
O L A S J A N G E L
```

Building a Church of Belonging and Welcome

Below is a survey, a way for you to measure the way you feel about something. Check the answers that are right for you. (Please remember that a survey is *not* a test. There are no wrong answers!)

1) I feel welcome at my church

_____ always

_____ sometimes

_____ never

2) Someone greets me at the front door of our church

_____ always

_____ sometimes

_____ never

3) People extend the Sign of Peace to one another

_____ with smiles

_____ with straight faces

_____ with frowns

4) After Mass at my church

_____ people race to their cars

_____ some people stay and talk

_____ we often have coffee and donuts or something

What did this survey tell you about how welcoming your church is?

Can you name at least five ways (people, events or things said to you) that made you feel welcomed at your church?

1)____

2)____

3)____

4)____

5)____

THE MAIDEN WHO FINALLY FOUND A HOME

Before You Meet

Read the material below and "The Maiden Who Finally Found a Home" in *Spirit With Us*.

Kateri Tekakwitha's life is known through a combination of journals written by Jesuit missionaries and stories told and retold by admirers. She blended the Native American ways of her people with the Christian teaching of the Blackrobes (Jesuits). Kateri Tekakwitha was a young woman of strength, faith and courage. She overcame much adversity to belong to the Christian family.

Theme. Belonging to a faith community gives us support and strength.

If, as we've already discussed, it is risky to talk about God, then it is even more scary to do what God wants us to do. But the Spirit makes sure we are never alone. Belonging to God and to the Church means we *have* a home and *are* a home for others, just like Kateri. There is challenge in following Jesus' Spirit, but there is safety and assurance as well.

Optional Activity. Our society tries in many ways to keep us safe. Visit a fire station, a police department or a hospital. Talk to people who work there about how they help others and support their colleagues at the same time.

Together Time

Set the Environment. Open with a prayer.

Getting Started. Who makes you feel safe and "at home"? Why? Where is your true home? Why?

Read the Story. The following questions may encourage discussion.

1) What was your favorite part of the story? Why?

2) Why was it so hard for Kateri to be baptized?

3) Have you ever wanted something as much as Kateri wanted to belong to the Christian family? What happened?

Activity. On the reverse is an activity for you to do separately and then bring together.

Closing Ritual. Native Americans teach us much about belonging. Tribal ties are unbreakable and constant, a family of unconditional love. All creation is united in importance, all life is respected. Ask Kateri Tekakwitha to help you take care of our world and all life upon it.

Welcome Home!

Some churches have a "Homecoming" or "Welcome" Sunday. This is a time when parishioners who have moved away, alienated Catholics and those still seeking a Church family are warmly invited to attend.

Pretend your church is having a "Welcome" Sunday and you are in charge of designing a banner for the front door.

- What is especially good (unique, valuable) about your church?

- How do the people in your church make others feel welcome?

- Why is it important for us as Christians to be a welcoming community?

After you have reflected on these questions and your child has completed the first activity, design your banner together. Remember, a banner has only a few words on it and uses color and design to catch the eye.

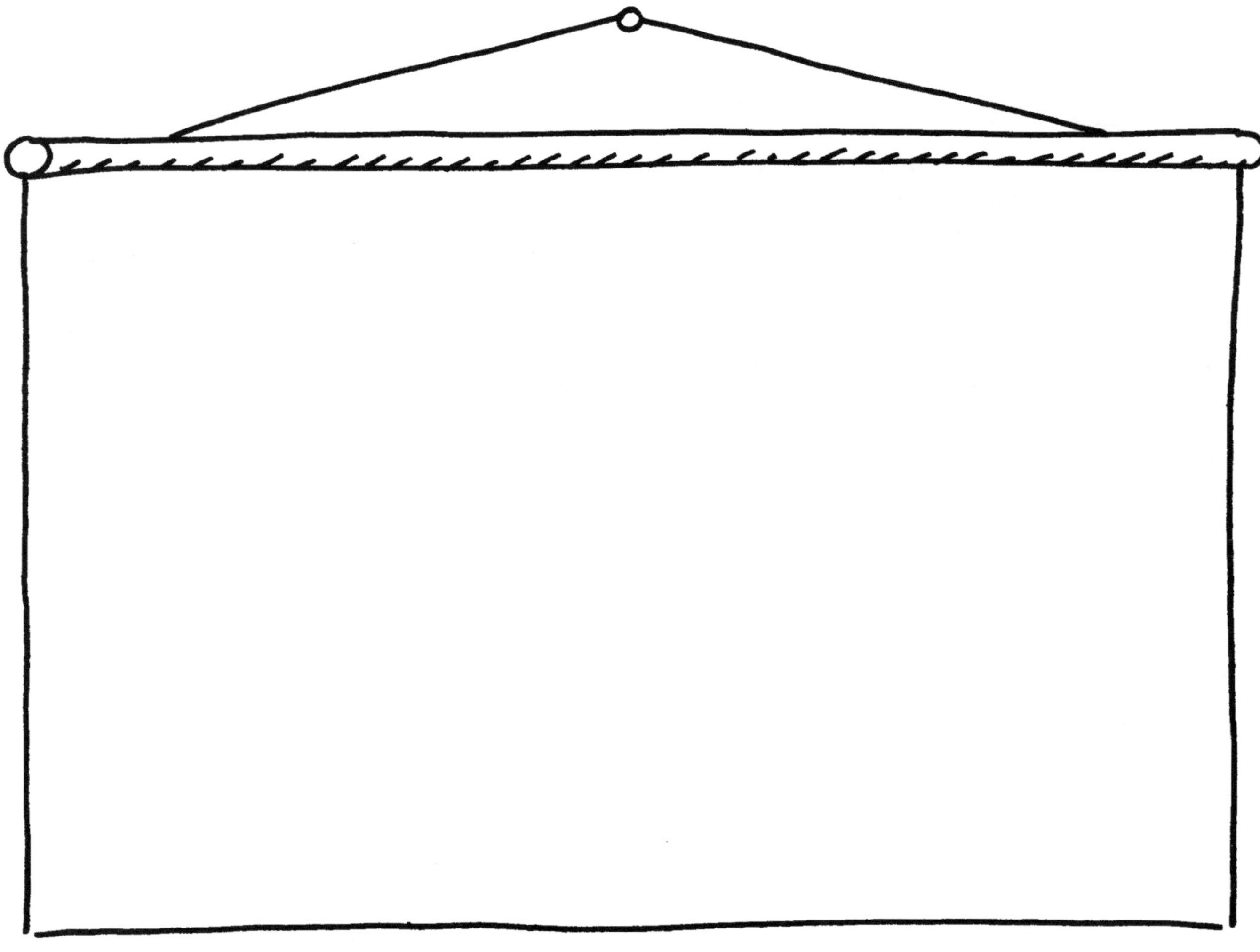

A Short but Rich Life

Kateri did not live long, but we still remember her today. She lived a life of great love for the Spirit.

The crossword puzzle below has many words from her life. See how many you remember from your reading!

ACROSS

1. Kateri Tekakwitha wanted very much to be ______.
3. Short for New York
4. Father ______ baptized Kateri.
6. The missionaries ______ and left too quickly to baptize Kateri at first.
7. Kateri was left with many ______ after her illness.
9. Her ______ was the chief.
10. Kateri wanted to feel __ home somewhere.
11. What we use to see
13. The disease that killed Kateri's family
16. Kateri's tribe

DOWN

1. What the Mohawks called the missionaries
2. Musical instruments
4. A member of the Society of Jesus
5. An organized body of people (Hint: look at #4 down.)
8. To move quickly
12. A popular breakfast food
14. The member of Kateri's family who was Catholic
15. Seat in a church

Finally Finding a Home

Kateri Tekakwitha struggled with wanting to belong and to feel at home. Eventually she found a place where she was welcomed.

Think about some words and actions that make people feel welcome. Then place these words or actions in the puzzle below, using one of the letters in the word *WELCOME* in each phrase. The letters may be used at the beginning, middle or end of the phrase. (For example, "hoW are you?" or "sMile.")

hoW are you?

E

L

C

O

sMile

E

W

E

L

C

O

M

E

SPIRIT OF PRAYER

Before You Meet

Read the material below. Read "Spirit of Prayer" in *Spirit With Us*.

Prayer is a very important dimension of living as a Christian. Prayer is both private and communal. Within these two broad categories are a great variety of options. Prayer is our response to God's love in our lives. The communal prayer central to our Catholic beliefs is the sacrament we call the Eucharist.

Theme. The Sacrament of the Eucharist nourishes our relationship with God. There are many different ways to spend time with God in prayer.

There are many ways to pray, but all of them require intention and awareness. We *choose* to spend time with God. Learning formal prayers helps us pray with others and to pray when our own words fail us. Spontaneous prayer, aloud or silent, can open our deepest needs to God's care. Praying in community, especially at Sunday Eucharist, helps us remember that we are part of a family and can help carry us through times of doubt or confusion. Whatever the type, prayer places us firmly in God's presence.

Optional Activity. Many prayer books and spiritual resources are available in libraries and bookstores. Start a small notebook with your favorite prayers in it. Ask for a tour of your church so you can see up close the building where the community gathers.

Together Time

Set the Environment. Open with a prayer.

Getting Started. What's the most fun you've had spending time with a friend? Why? Is there someplace where it's easier for you to pray? Why? What do you like about praying?

Read the Story. The follow questions may encourage discussion.

1) Is there someplace where it's easier for you to pray? Why?

2) What do you like about praying?

Activity. On the next page is an activity for you to do together.

Closing Ritual. Eucharist uses the important symbols of bread and wine, which become the Body and Blood of Christ. Place some snack to share between you. Then say whatever form of grace before meals you wish. As you eat, talk about how Jesus ate with his friends, too. Close with the doxology: "Through Jesus, in Jesus, and with Jesus, in the unity of the Holy Spirit, all glory and honor is yours, Almighty Father, forever and ever. Amen."

Jesus as Our Model of Prayer

In Scripture we see that Jesus prayed in many different ways. Look up the Scripture readings below. Make a list of the ways you notice Jesus praying. Then make up a second list of the ways you can use Jesus as a model for your own prayer.

Matthew 3:13-17	Mark 6 41-44
Matthew 6:5-15	Luke 4:14-21
Matthew 14:22-24	Luke 22:39-46
Mark 1:35-37	John 17:9-23

Jesus prayed by	**We can do this by**

THE CHURCH AT HOME

Before You Meet

Read the material below. Read "The Church at Home" in *Spirit With Us*.

Nympha and the Church in her house are mentioned in Colossians 4:15. There is evidence that the early gatherings of the followers of Christ were held in what we call "house churches." Those who had homes large enough would host these celebrations. This story is a fictionalized account of what one of these early Eucharists might have been like.

Theme. The most special time we gather with others to pray is the Sunday Eucharist.

In the Gospels, Jesus commissioned Christians to "do this in remembrance of me." The Sunday Eucharist can be traced back to these gospel times.

Eucharist is still the greatest source of grace and nourishment for our community. At Mass we receive the Body and Blood of Christ, and we reclaim our title as "the Body of Christ."

Optional Activity. Discuss the upcoming or recent Sunday readings. Look for whatever "food for thought" you may find. Volunteer some time or somehow support a program in your community that feeds the poor.

Together Time

Set the Environment. Open with a prayer.

Getting Started. What was the best party you ever attended? What made it so?

Read the Story. The following questions may encourage discussion.

1) What was your favorite part of the story? Why?

2) If you were Nympha, what would you want to do to get ready?

3) Can you think of ways to make your meals with family or friends into times when you also remember the Body of Christ? How?

Activity. On the next page is an activity for you to do separately and then bring together.

Closing Ritual. Read aloud from another of Paul's Letters, 1 Corinthians 11:23-26. Then answer your invitation from Jesus by finishing this prayer: "Thanks for inviting me, Jesus. I look forward to your party because...."

The Pleasure of Your Company Is Requested

Have you ever heard Mass compared to a party or a dinner? There are many similarities because both are meals.

Sunday Eucharist is divided into two main parts: the Liturgy of the Word and the Liturgy of the Eucharist. These are sandwiched between the Introductory and Closing Rites. The Liturgy of the Word, where we hear the readings and the homily, is not unlike that time period at any party where people catch up with each other. We hear the stories of our tradition, the Good News of Jesus, and applications to our lives.

The Liturgy of the Eucharist is an even more obvious parallel. We bring forward the bread and wine. The table (altar) is set. The meal is prepared (Eucharistic Prayer). We all eat. Indeed, we may even watch the presider do the dishes!

Reflect on your experiences of Mass.

With your young person, fill out the invitation below together. Decorate the invitation in any way you like.

When you finish, hang your invitation somewhere (perhaps on the refrigerator) to remind you that this is an ongoing party and all are welcome!

An Invitation

You are cordially invited to a special gathering of friends!

Who is invited:

When:

Where:

Why:

Guest of honor:

What you will bring:

See you soon!
Love,
Jesus

RSVP

What Do You Mean Mass Is a Party?

Think about it for a moment: What do you see happening at Mass?

There are two main parts of the Mass: the Liturgy of the Word and the Liturgy of the Eucharist. And there are things that happen within these two that closely resemble a meal or a party.

See if you can match up the party activities with parts of the Mass most like them by putting the appropriate letters in the blanks:

A. Eating the food

B. Hearing all the family news

C. Bringing food to share

D. Being welcomed by the host

E. Apologizing to anyone there whom you have hurt

F. Preparing the food to eat

G. Relaxing afterward (and thanking the hosts)

H. Getting some good advice from a friend

I. Worrying about those who are not there, or remembering them with affection

Introductory Rites

___ Greeting by priest/presider

___ Penitential Rite

Liturgy of the Word

___ Readings and Gospel

___ Homily

___ Prayer of the Faithful (General Intercessions)

Liturgy of the Eucharist

___ Preparation of Gifts (Offertory)

___ Eucharistic Prayer

___ Communion

___ Prayer After Communion

Your Invitation to Jesus

With your adult partner, you will fill out an invitation from Jesus to Sunday Eucharist. Good manners, however, means we often invite to our party those who have invited us to theirs. So let's say you "owe" Jesus an invitation. The sentence stems below are to help you decide where and when and to what you would like to invite Jesus.

The place I'd most like to have a party is ___________________________________

____.

The food I would serve is ____

____.

The music I would play is ____

____.

The decorations would be ____

____.

The people I would invite (besides Jesus) are ________________________________

____.

The time of year I would have the party is ___________________________________

____.

The time of day I would have it is ____

____.

The reason I want Jesus to come to this party is ______________________________

____.

THE WOMAN WHO LAUGHED WITH GOD

Before You Meet

Read the materials below. Read "The Woman Who Laughed with God" in *Spirit With Us.*

Sister Thea Bowman is a woman of our recent history. She died at 53 years of age in 1990. In her short life she accomplished many things. Sister Thea was a respected teacher, an engaging preacher and a persuasive voice for respect among different cultures. Her obvious love of God and of others made the Spirit of Jesus manifest for people all over the world. Sister Thea's joy even in the dark times of her illness is probably the thing most remembered about her.

Theme. When we pray individually, we bring back to God the rich diversity of creation.

If we limit ourselves to one way to pray, the way most common to our culture, we will lose opportunities to grow in our awareness of God. We are created as individuals who bring our own experiences, background and stories to our prayers. The beauty of the Spirit of Jesus lies in our recognition of the diversity of humanity. There are many ways to pray!

Optional Activity. Talk with a variety of people about when they most like to pray and how they pray. This group could include your pastor, a pastor from another tradition, members of your family, your Church or other faiths. Go to the library and see if you can rent a video or borrow a prayer book from another faith tradition. How are we different? How are we alike?

Together Time

Set the Environment. Open with a prayer.

Getting Started. What makes you laugh? Has there ever been a time when you "laughed with God" because you were so happy? What happened?

Read the Story. The following questions may encourage discussion.

1) What is your favorite part of the story? Why?

2) Why do you think God made us so different? What do you like most about yourself?

3) When do you do your best praying? Where? Alone or with others?

Activity. On the following page is an activity that you and your young person will do separately.

Closing Ritual. Bring your activity sheets together. Think of a song you could both listen to and reflect upon in this ritual. Where is God in the lyrics of this music? Thank God for all our differences and for the rich diversity in our world!

How Do You Pray?

There are many ways to pray, and we use them at different times. Sister Thea was very clear in her message to us: It is not important *how* we pray. It *is* important *that* we pray.

Please look at the list below (your young person has a similar list). How many of these "ways of prayer" have you tried?

1) Place a check mark by any of these you have tried.

2) Place a star by the ones you like best.

3) Place a question mark by the ones you would like to try.

_______ Journaling (writing down your thoughts, prayers or

observations)

_______ Walking outside in nature

_______ Sunday Mass

_______ Weekday Mass

_______ Talking with God

_______ Saying the rosary

_______ Sitting alone at home

_______ Singing

_______ Reading the Bible

_______ Listening to music

_______ Helping out others

_______ Listening to a friend

_______ Other (please describe)

Who We Are, Whose We Are

Sister Thea used to say "Always remember who you are and whose you are."

   Using the color code below, fill in the spaces in the heart. Inside the heart is the answer to Sister Thea's reminder.

3 = red   7 = yellow

Many Ways to Pray

There are many ways to pray. Some may not even seem like praying, but they are.
   Read the list below. (Your adult partner has the same list.) Put an X next to the
ways you have prayed.
   Place a star (*) by the one you like best.
   Place a question mark (?) by the ones you might like to try.

______ Journaling (writing down your thoughts, prayers or observations)

______ Walking outside in nature

______ Sunday Mass

______ Weekday Mass

______ Talking with God

______ Saying the rosary

______ Sitting alone at home

______ Singing

______ Reading the Bible

______ Listening to music

______ Helping others out

______ Listening to a friend

______ Other (please describe)

SPIRIT OF FORGIVENESS

Before You Meet

Read the materials below. Read "Spirit of Forgiveness" in *Spirit With Us.*

Along with "please" and "thank you," "I'm sorry" is one of the first things we learn to say as children. The ability to be forgiven and to forgive others is important to relationships and families. It is important to our relationship with God as well. We believe that God is always ready to forgive us when we ask. (Please look to the Appendix, page 57, for more specific information on the Sacrament of Reconciliation.)

Theme. The Sacrament of Reconciliation is the Church's celebration of God's mercy and forgiveness.

First we have to admit we have done something wrong. Then we have to apologize to those we hurt. Finally, we have to change our ways to avoid doing the same wrong again. If we are the ones receiving the apology, we need to risk forgiving that person. The two stories in this section both talk about how we ask for forgiveness and how we give forgiveness to others.

Optional Activity. Many family-appropriate videos and movies deal with forgiveness. Find one you would like to see with your young person. (*Beauty and the Beast, Mighty Ducks, Field of Dreams, Clara's Heart* are just a few.) Also notice what your friends and family members do when they want to be forgiven. Do you have any personal rituals of reconciliation like a hug or a special phrase you say?

Together Time

Set the Environment. Open with a prayer.

Getting Started. When was the last time you had to say "I'm sorry"? When was the last time you had to forgive someone?

Read the Story. The following questions may encourage discussion.

1) How do you feel when you have made a mistake or even hurt someone? What do you do?

2) Are there any people you feel you can't forgive? Why? What would make it possible for you to forgive them?

Activity. On the reverse is an activity for you and your young person to do together.

Closing Ritual. Placing your "circles of hurt" in front of you, say this prayer: "God of mercy, we ask for your forgiveness. Teach us how to forgive others. We ask this through Jesus, in Jesus, and with Jesus, in the unity of the Holy Spirit, forever and ever. Amen."

Circles of Hurt, Ripples of Sin

Before we can talk about forgiveness, we have to recognize the reality of sin. We all make mistakes, and when we deliberately are selfish or hurt others, these mistakes become sin.

We call the time when we look at our lives to identify sinful actions an "examination of conscience." That means we examine, or look at closely, the inner voice and thoughts that tell us when we have done something wrong.

Hurtful things have a way of "rippling out" to others. We hurt someone in our family circle, and they take their anger to work or school. Then they hurt someone there! So, just like a pebble dropped in a lake, one sin can spread out to hurt many, many other people.

It happens in the other direction as well! For example, a government may cut funding for school breakfasts, so a particular school has to stop offering help to its children. Then a child in that school may go hungry all day because there is no food at home.

Below are three circles, one for family and friends, one for our community and one for our world. List in each circle the hurts that happen, on purpose or unintentionally. (You'll notice at the end how each one can "ripple" into the other!)

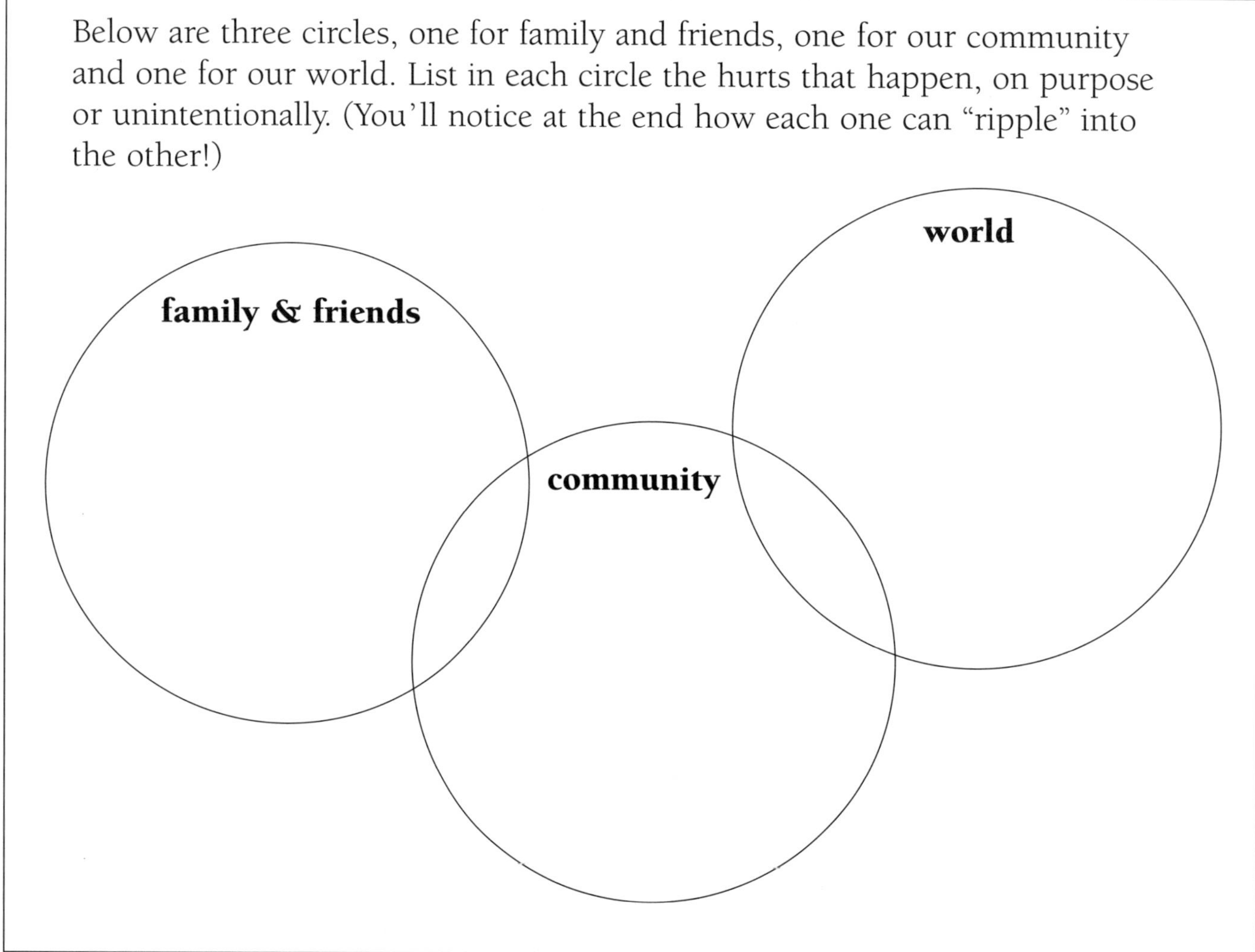

THE MAN WHO MADE TROUBLE

Before You Meet

Read the materials below. Read "The Man Who Made Trouble" in *Spirit With Us.*

The story of Paul's conversion is in the ninth chapter of the Acts of the Apostles. The Saul we read about early in Acts is certainly different from the Paul of the later chapters or the Paul we know through his Letters in the New Testament! The difference is Paul's acceptance of Jesus' loving forgiveness, even after he had imprisoned Jesus' followers.

Theme. Each of us sometimes does wrong and must ask for forgiveness.

If Paul can change from angry persecutor to powerful preacher, think how much can happen through the power of the Spirit! We all get second chances; we all get to begin again. This is a wonderful and liberating truth of our faith. God will always forgive us our sins because God is always ready to love us. Sin blinds us, just as Paul was blind, but forgiveness makes us well. It is not without good reason that we recognize Reconciliation as a Sacrament of Healing.

Optional Activity. Visit the Reconciliation Room at your church if you have one. What about this space makes it comfortable or welcoming? What would make it more welcoming?

Talk about some of the programs in your community that offer people a second chance (such as halfway houses, hospitals, Twelve Step programs, soup kitchens). Visit one if possible, and talk to a volunteer there about forgiveness and second chances.

Together Time

Set the Environment. Open with a prayer.

Getting Started. When was the last time you knew you had a second chance, a chance to change and improve? What happened?

Read the Story. The following questions may encourage discussion.

1) What is your favorite part of the story? Why?

2) If you had been Ananias, what would you have thought about Paul? What would you have done? Why?

3) How do you think Paul felt when he knew he had been wrong to imprison the Christians? Pretend you are Paul. What would you say to the Christians? What would you say to the people in Jerusalem who sent you to capture the Christians?

Activity. On the next page is a prayer service that you and your young person will prepare for separately.

Closing Ritual. Pray together the prayer service on the top of your activity sheet. You will need a Bible or children's Bible.

Saying 'I'm Sorry' and Being Forgiven

If we never have the experience of being forgiven, how will we be able to forgive others? Answer the reflection questions, and then come together with your young person to share this prayer service. Be open to the reality that we can *all* experience forgiveness because our loving God is waiting for us to come home.

Reflection Questions

To prepare for the Prayer Service, look back at the circles of hurt from the last activity page. Using these "sins" as your guide, finish these sentences:

"I'm sorry ____."

"We need you God, to ____."

"I will never again ____."

Prayer of Reconciliation

Opening Prayer:

"In the name of the Father, and of the Son, and of the Holy Spirit. Amen."

Reading: 2 Corinthians 5:17-19

Response: Take turns sharing your reflections by finishing this sentence:

"Lord, we are sorry that we _______________________________________."

Prayer of Sorrow: *(Adult leads; young person responds "Amen.")*

"God of loving mercy,
we are not perfect people,
but we are trying to be your followers.
Help us to admit when we do wrong.
Lead us to reconcile with others.
Guide us to healing the world with your justice and peace.
We ask all this through, with, and in Jesus and the Holy Spirit. Amen."

Closing Blessing: *(Raise your right hands over one another's heads.)*

"As Ananias touched Paul and his sight returned,
let your forgiveness, Lord, bless us and heal us. Amen."

Sign of Peace: Close by exchanging a sign of Christ's peace.

A Message From Paul

Paul wrote many letters to the Christian communities he helped start. But what has happened here? It looks like Paul's pages became separated and are out of order.

Can you number the sentences so they will make sense again?

______ "Being blinded actually let me see what I couldn't see before, that Jesus of Nazareth is indeed the Messiah and Savior!"

______ "I stood and watched them stone Stephen, and I knew then that I wanted to see all the followers of Christ be punished."

______ "So I asked the voice in the brightness, who are you? And it answered 'Jesus.'"

______ "They actually had to lower me down the wall in a basket, that's how angry some in Damascus had become! But I got away."

______ "I went to Damascus determined to imprison as many followers of Jesus as I could before returning to Jerusalem."

______ "There was this incredibly bright light and loud voice that knocked me to the ground!"

______ "At first, they wondered why I was preaching about Jesus, I who had so persecuted those who believed in him."

______ "When I regained my sight, I knew I had to start telling everyone that Jesus is Lord."

Asking for Forgiveness

We learn how to forgive others by being forgiven ourselves. If we think we are too good to need forgiveness, we can begin to think too highly of ourselves and think that others are beneath us. If we think we are so bad we can never be forgiven, then we are denying our own goodness, which comes directly from God.

   None of us is perfect, but all of us belong to our forgiving God.

Reflection Questions

To prepare for the prayer service, look back at the circles of hurt on the last Together Page. Using these "sins" as your guide, finish these sentences:

   "I'm sorry, God, that I ____."

   "I need your help, God, because ____."

   "Something I will never again do is ____."

You may not know it, but you have just written a prayer. This kind of prayer is called an "Act of Sorrow" or an "Act of Contrition."

Here is an Act of Sorrow you can learn by heart and use if you wish:

>O my God,
>I am sorry for all my sins,
>because they displease you,
>who are worthy of all my love.
>With your help, I will sin no more.
>Amen.

THE SOLDIER WHO HAD NO ENEMIES

Before You Meet

Read the materials below. Read "The Soldier Who Had No Enemies" in *Spirit With Us.*

Saint Maximilian Kolbe was martyred during World War II. This terrible war revealed much about how cruel humans can be. But Maximilian's life was a testament to the best humanity can be in spite of evil. His acceptance of others, his relentless faith and his courageous actions were all clear signs of the Spirit of Christ in his life. Maximilian's special devotion to Mary, the mother of Jesus, led him to value fidelity and forgiveness. His ability to forgive others challenges us today!

Theme. We are called by the Spirit of God to forgive others.

It is not easy to forgive. We are much more likely to try to strike back or hold grudges. Forgiveness requires that we let go of our hurt. Such Christian forgiveness is a gift of the Holy Spirit. (See Appendix for the list of the Gifts of the Holy Spirit.) This type of love is heroic indeed.

Optional Activity. Look up the history of some troubled spot in today's world (any country at war within itself or with another country). What brought the two sides to this conflict? What could genuine forgiveness do?

Together Time

Set the Environment. Open with a prayer.

Getting Started. Did you ever have a very hard time forgiving someone else? How did it turn out? How do you feel about it now?

Read the Story. The following questions may encourage discussion.

1) What is your favorite part of the story? Why?

2) Do you think Maximilian Kolbe was brave? Why? Have you seen any of this kind of bravery in yourself? When?

3) When is it hard for you to forgive? How do you feel after you have forgiven someone?

Activity. On the next page is an activity that you and your young person will do separately.

Closing Ritual. Forgiveness means letting go. Take the initials, names and events you wrote down during your activity time and rip them up into little pieces. Ask God to help you let them go.

The Freedom and the Courage to Forgive

Go back to your circles of hurt one last time. Are there hurts or sins in one of those circles that are especially hard for you to forgive in yourself? In others? What are they?

Why are these hard for you to forgive?

Is it harder for you to forgive sin in yourself or in others? Why?

Just as the balloons in the drawing below are being released into the sky, so we, too, can ask God to help us release our anger, hurt or disappointment so we may truly forgive ourselves and others.

Take a separate piece of paper (you'll be ripping it up during the Closing Ritual) and write a letter to God. Ask God for the strength or gifts you need to be forgiving. It may also be helpful to tell God exactly what hurts you about this sin and how you feel about the one who hurt you. (God can take hearing our anger and pain. Remember Jesus in the Garden of Gethsemane!) This letter will not be read by anyone else.

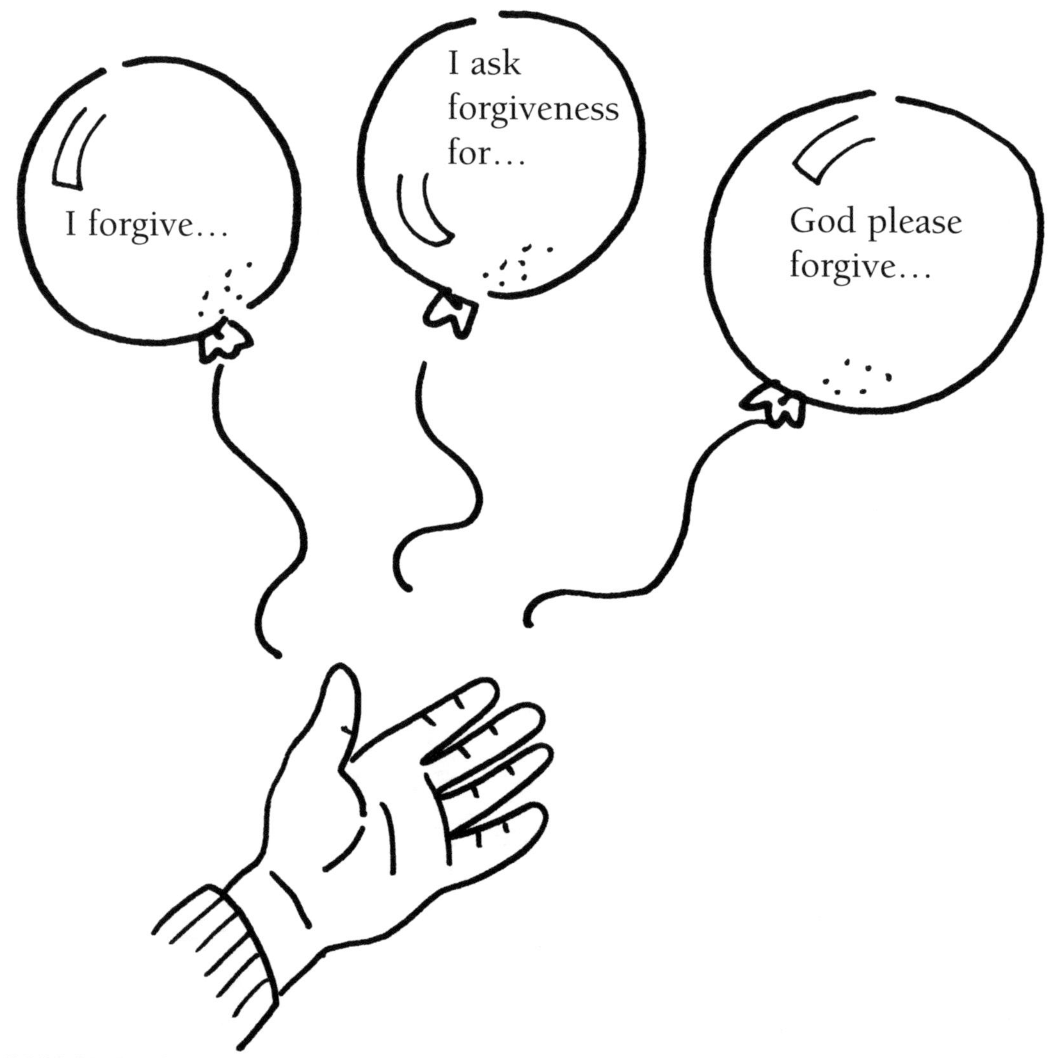

Changing to Happy Endings

Can you suggest a new ending to either of these stories? How could forgiveness help these people?

Susie is very angry. She called Judi to ask her to a movie, and Judi said she was sick. But when Susie showed up at the theater, there sat Judi and Rita! "I'm never going to ask her again," Susie thought. But really, Susie was sad enough to cry. Just then, Judi turned around and saw Susie. Judi was too embarrassed to say anything. "I bet she'll never speak to me again," Judi worried.

For the last two weeks at school, neither of them has spoken to the other. And Susie is always making fun of Rita.

____

____

____

____

____.

Levon and Darrell have known each other since kindergarten. Levon is the better athlete, but both of them have always enjoyed playing basketball. When they had try-outs for the team this year, Darrell was afraid he wouldn't make the team. He asked Levon to ask the coach to let Darrell play. "He needs your talent," Darrell told Levon, "just tell him you'll quit if I don't make the team. Then he'll have to let me on!"

Levon felt that really wasn't the right thing to do, but he didn't know how to tell Darrell what he really thought. When the team list was posted without Darrell's name on it, he came to Levon shouting, "I thought you weren't going to play without me!" Levon just walked away quietly. "And I thought you were my real friend," Levon murmured to himself. Now both avoid each other.

____

____

____

____.

Forgiving Means Letting Go

We have already talked about asking for forgiveness. Saint Maximilian Kolbe teaches us that we must also be ready to forgive others.

Just as we can let go of helium balloons and watch them float upward through the sky, so we need to let go of our anger and hurt. When we do that, we are then ready to forgive others. To whom do we let them go? To God, of course!

In each of the balloons below, write a word or initials to represent some event or person you are ready to forgive. If you need more balloons, draw them on this page.

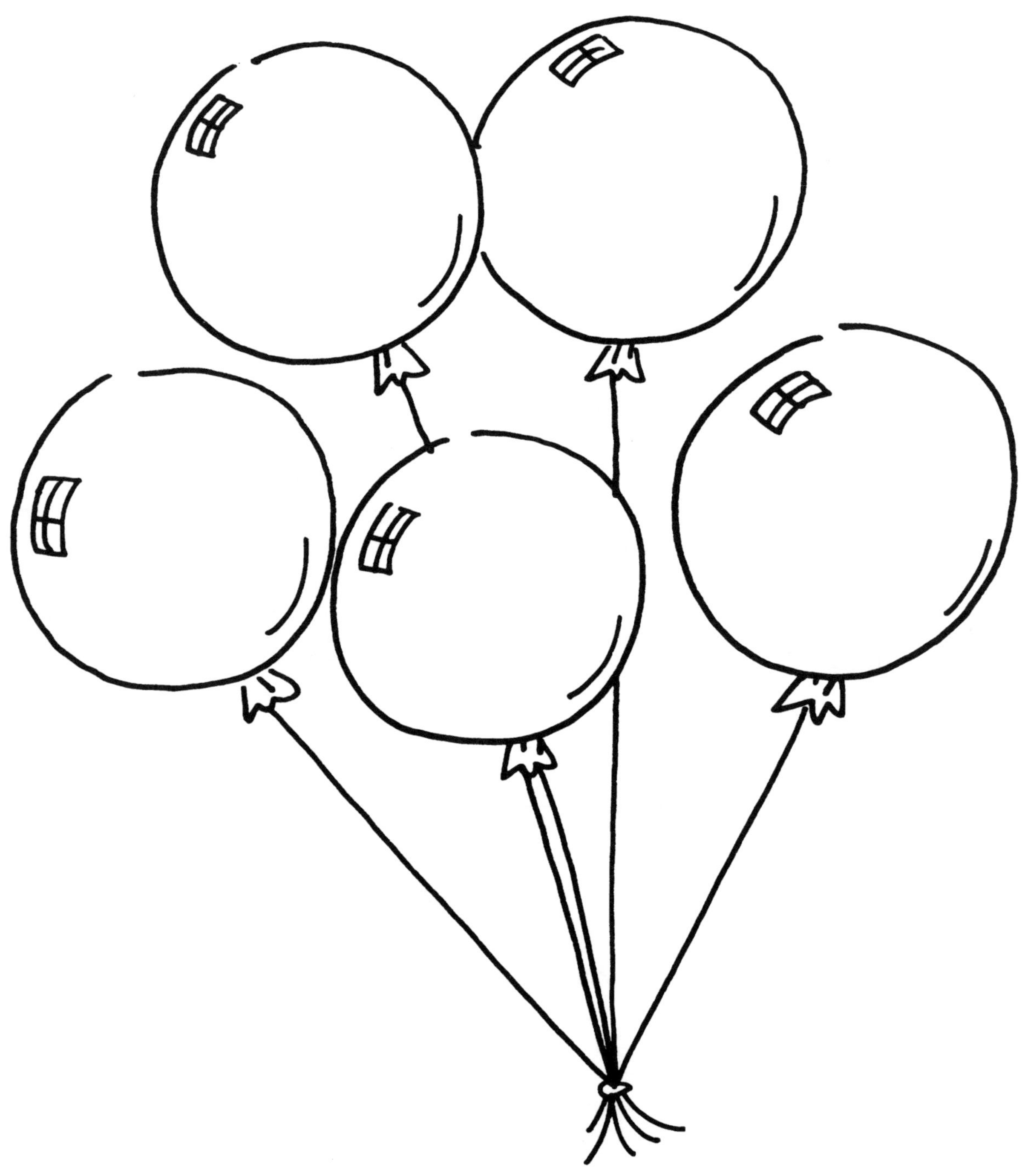

SPIRIT OF ACTION

Before You Meet

Read the materials below. Read "Spirit of Action" in *Spirit With Us.*

Confirmation is intricately linked with the Sacrament of Baptism. For the earliest Christians these two, combined with the Sacrament of Eucharist, were the one sacrament that initiated new members. As they evolved into separate rites in the Roman Church, they also developed unique understandings. Today we are making an effort to reestablish the crucial link between Baptism and Confirmation.

Theme. The Sacrament of Confirmation reaffirms our baptismal call to *act* to help establish the Reign of God.

Being a Christian is work—sometimes hard work indeed. But the Spirit's message of hope is twofold: We are never alone in our efforts; we are never without God. Confirmation is yet another chance for the Spirit to enter our lives, bringing God's grace. And once we have received the Spirit, we can no longer sit quiet and still. We must speak and we must act.

Optional Activity. Go over the list of the Holy Spirit's gifts in the Appendix. Decide which of these gifts are important to you for their ability to give you the strength to act. Which gifts do you still need to work on? Make a mobile of the words to hang in your meeting space. As the wind moves the mobile, notice how strong something you can't see (like an air current) can be. What does this mobile say to you about the Spirit?

Together Time

Set the Environment. Open with a prayer.

Getting Started. When have you surprised yourself by the way you were acting? What was going on? How did you feel later?

Read the Story. The following questions may encourage discussion.

1) Do you try to say what you mean and do what you say? Give an example.

2) Are there times when you think people are telling you one thing but doing another? How does this make you feel?

3) What is your favorite gift of the Spirit? Why?

Activity. On the next page is an activity that you and your young person will do together.

Closing Ritual. Make the Sign of the Cross on each other's hands, eyes and lips. As you make these three signs of blessing, say, "Through Jesus [hands], with Jesus [eyes] and in Jesus [lips], in the unity of the Holy Spirit, all glory and honor is yours, Almighty Father, forever and ever. Amen."

Acting Out the Plan of God

We are all gifted, just gifted differently. And that is good, because that means we all have something to contribute to the Reign of God.

Jesus counts on us! Together, *we* are the Body of Christ!

In the spaces below, list some ways you can be the Body of Christ.

How I can be the eyes of Jesus (how I see the world):_______________________

____

____

How I can be the lips of Jesus (what I say to others):_______________________

____

____

How I can be the hands of Jesus (what I give or do):_______________________

____

____

How I can be the feet of Jesus (how far
and where I am willing to go):

____

____

____

How I can be the heart of
Jesus (how I show love):

____

____

A Letter of Good News

Before You Meet

Read the materials. Read "The Letter of Good News" in *Spirit With Us.*

The Letter of James is in the New Testament. It was written for the Jewish Christian community in Jerusalem. Its message is simple but clear: Faith, true faith, requires good works. James was reminding his community (and reminds us today) that each of us is called to be Christian in action as well as in belief.

Theme. Each of us can work individually toward justice and compassion in many ways.

The evils of the world can seem overwhelming, but James reminds us that we can and must start right where we are! The people closest to us, our family and our friends, are where we first need to live the Gospel message of love, forgiveness and peace. No one is too young, too weak or too slow to answer this call of the Spirit.

Optional Activity. Many saints of our tradition felt that the day-to-day events of our lives were the ground of holiness. The lives of Saint Therese (the Little Flower), Saint Francis of Assisi, Thomas Merton, Mother Teresa and others were filled with appreciation for the details of our lives.

Find a simple activity you and your young person can do together: Pick up litter, take cans to a recycling center, drop off clothes at a thrift shop, and so on.

Together Time

Set the Environment. Open with a prayer.

Getting Started. Was there a time when someone did a small act of kindness or said a comforting word that made a big difference to you? Share your story.

Read the Story. The following questions may encourage discussion.

1) What is your favorite part of the story? Why?

2) Can you name some of the evils or sins that James was observing? Why did these make him so sad?

3) Have you ever felt like James? That is, do you ever wonder why people do mean or evil things to each other? What would you like to say to them if you had the chance?

Activity. Following is an activity that you and your young person will do separately and bring together.

Closing Ritual. Read together James 2:14-17. Then read the commitments from your Together Pages. Close by thanking the Spirit for the gifts that enable you to keep these commitments.

Responding to James's Letter of Good News

In the last activity, you listed some ways you could be the eyes, lips, hands, feet and heart of Jesus. But, as James writes, it is only when we put these commitments into action that we are truly living as Christians!

Look back over your ideas from the previous activity and commit yourself to a course of action. (Your young person is doing the same thing.) Remember that just as evil can start small and ripple out to many, so can peace and compassion start in our own hearts and families and extend to all we meet!

I will be the *eyes* of Jesus because I will

____

____

_______________________.

I will be the *heart* of Jesus because I will

____

____

_______________________.

I will be the *lips* of Jesus because I will

____

____

____

I will be the *hands* of Jesus because I will

____

____

_______________________.

I will be the *feet* of Jesus because I will

____

____

_______________________.

And we will do all this through the gifts of the Spirit with us.

After you have both finished your reflection, each of you initial the part of the Body of Christ you will try to be.

Figuring Out the Good News

Can you crack this simple substitution code? When you do, you will find a message from James about the importance of the Spirit of Action!
  (There's a hint in small print at the bottom if you really need it!)

UZRGS DRGSLFG DLIPH RH WVZW!

_ _ _ _ _   _ _ _ _ _ _ _

_ _ _ _ _   _ _   _ _ _ _ _!

(HINT: Z=A)

Responding to James's Letter of Good News

In the last activity, you listed some ways you could be the eyes, lips, hands, feet and heart of Jesus. But, as James writes, it is only when we put these commitments into action that we are truly living as Christians!

Look back over your ideas from the previous activity and commit yourself to one course of action. (Your adult is doing the same thing.) Remember that just as evil can start small and ripple out to many, so can peace and compassion start in our own hearts and families and extend to all we meet!

I will be the *eyes* of Jesus because I will

____

____________________.

I will be the *hands* of Jesus because I will

____

____

____________________.

I will be the *heart* of Jesus because I will

____

____________________.

I will be the *feet* of Jesus because I will

____

____________________.

I will be the *lips* of Jesus because I will

____

____

And we will do all this through the gifts of the Spirit with us.

THE BISHOP FOR THE POOR

Before You Meet

Read the materials below. Read "The Bishop for the Poor" in *Spirit With Us.*

The Catholic Churches of Central and South America have given much to their northern neighbors. Small faith-sharing communities, liberation theology and many examples of courageous martyrdom have profoundly affected the universal Church. Archbishop Oscar Romero, his life and his example, certainly fit into this list of shared graces. His real-life story has more drama than many fiction pieces and more to teach us than this short treatment can reveal.

Theme. As a community, as a Church, we are involved in bringing about the Reign of God in our world.

Not only as individuals but also as members of an institution, we are called to act for the Reign of God. In fact, there is a power in "us" that "I" alone cannot capture. Archbishop Romero never stopped loving his community and its tradition. It was on this firm foundation that he accomplished his ministry. This is how the Spirit works for us as well, within the structure of our community and our Church.

Optional Activity. Investigate what your parish offers in the way of social action. Many parishes have food pantries, outreach programs or cooperative events with social agencies. Find a way to get involved.

Together Time

Set the Environment. Open with a prayer.

Getting Started. Has some event in your life ever changed the way you think or feel about things? Why did this happen?

Read the Story. The following questions may encourage discussion.

1) What is your favorite part of the story? Why?

2) Do you agree with what Archbishop Romero decided? Why or why not?

3) Is there anything you would be willing to die for? What?

Activity. On the next pages is an activity that you and your young person will begin separately and finish together.

Closing Ritual. Share your "Daily Good News" papers. Ask God to bless and bring peace to people who are at war in the world, in their families and in themselves.

Bad News, Good News

Look through a paper or magazine. First you will probably notice the bad news—and most of it on the front page. But if you look deeper into the paper or periodical, you may find good news as well.

Use these pieces of good news (heroic people, happy events, moments of compassion and so on) to fill in the newspaper below with your young person. Children will also be looking for something for the *Daily Good News* in their activity.

The Reign of God

Archbishop Romero felt that there are two goals for Christians. One is to live with our eyes on heaven and the other is to live here on earth. God, for Oscar Romero, is best served right here and now.

Jesus tells us in Scripture what the Reign of God is like. It is like a mustard seed, a wedding banquet, a lost coin, a pearl of great value and many other images. This means that our imagination is important for helping the Reign of God happen. We have to be able to imagine a better world.

Using your imagination, what do you think the Reign of God is like? What images would you use to talk to modern people your age? (For example, "The Reign of God is like a compact disc, beautiful and nearly indestructible.")

The Reign of God is like ____

____

____.

The Reign of God is like ____

____

____.

The Reign of God is like ____

____

____.

The Reign of God is like ____

____

____.

The Reign of God is like ____

____

____.

Local Good News

You have read the story of Archbishop Oscar Romero, so you know how powerful it can be when people of faith join together.

You and your adult helper will be putting together a newspaper, *The Daily Good News*. You've just been hired as a stringer for this paper. (A "stringer" is an independent writer who goes after special stories.) Your assignment is to write in the space below some answers for these questions:

- When were you involved in some good news?
- What project have you worked on that succeeded?
- Whom have you helped lately?

You may write this story as an interview with yourself or someone else, as a straight report, or even as an editorial (an opinion piece).

THE NOT-THE-END

Before You Meet

Read the materials below. Read "The Not-the-End" in *Spirit With Us*.

The title of this series is *Spirit With Us*. If the stories you have shared with your young person do anything, they should show you that the Spirit is still active, still needed, still loving. Nothing is finished; all is still in process. We are continuing on our journey to God and to the Reign of God no matter what our age.

Theme. We are sacraments, individually and in community, because we continue to show the Spirit of God in our actions and our lives.

While we learn much from our study of Scripture and our examination of the lives of other committed Christians, we must also reflect on our own lives, our own stories. Help your young person finish the blank pages in this book. Help your children see the value of their own stories of faith. Help them see the action of the Spirit, who is indeed with us, in their lives.

Optional Activity. The best way to help your young persons value their own stories is for you to share your story of faith with them. Take time to reflect on where you have seen God and the Spirit act in your life.

Together Time

Set the Environment. Open with a prayer.

Getting Started. Who is the best storyteller in your family or among friends? Why?

Read the Story. The following questions may encourage discussion.

1) Do you believe that your story is as important as anyone's in the book? Why or why not?

2) What was your favorite story in *"Spirit With Us"*? Why?

Activity. On the next page is an activity for you to do. Your young person has empty pages in the book for his or her story as the closing activity.

Closing Ritual. Since this is your last session, close by sharing a meal or a special snack. As you eat, tell each other your "Not-the-End" stories. At the end of your time together, pray the doxology one more time: "Through Jesus, in Jesus, and with Jesus, in the unity of the Holy Spirit, all glory and honor is yours, Almighty Father, forever and ever. Amen." Remember to pray for each other whenever you hear those words at Sunday Mass.

Your Story of the Spirit

A story—or many stories—makes up the fabric of our lives. Remember the weaving activity at the beginning of this book? That was to remind you that your story is just as important as any other story in this book.

Take a few minutes now to think of your story. You may wish to share your thoughts with your young person.

I see the Spirit of belonging in my life in

____

____

I see the Spirit of prayer in my life in

____

____

I see the Spirit of forgiveness in my life in

____

____

I see the Spirit of action in my life in

____

____

My Story

On the remaining pages, write and draw the story of the Spirit at work in your life.

APPENDIX

The Rite of Reconciliation

The Sacrament of Reconciliation is a simple but important ritual. We celebrate God's love and forgiveness and the forgiving love of our community every time we receive this sacrament.

Individual Penance consists of just a few simple steps:

1) Greet and be welcomed by the priest.

2) Share a short Scripture reading chosen by the penitent or suggested by the confessor.

3) Confess your sins. Remember that this must be held in complete secrecy by the priest. Nothing you say will shock or surprise him. He is there as God's ear and God's healing presence.

4) Receive your penance. A penance is a way to show you are truly sorry and want to change so that you will not commit this sin again. It is usually an action or a prayer.

5) Say a prayer of sorrow. See the Adult's Together Page (page 32) or use your own words.

6) Receive absolution and give a sign of peace.

The Seven Gifts of the Holy Spirit

Wisdom, understanding, counsel, fortitude, knowledge, piety and fear of the Lord.

Answer Pages

Speaking in Tongues (page 7)

1) Apostles 2) Holy Spirit 3) Reign of God
4) Pentecost 5) Salvation 6) Ascension
7) Disciples 8) Peter 9) Mary

Within a Circle of Friends (page 10)

Father; Son; Holy Spirit; Amen.

Searching for the Right Words (page 13)

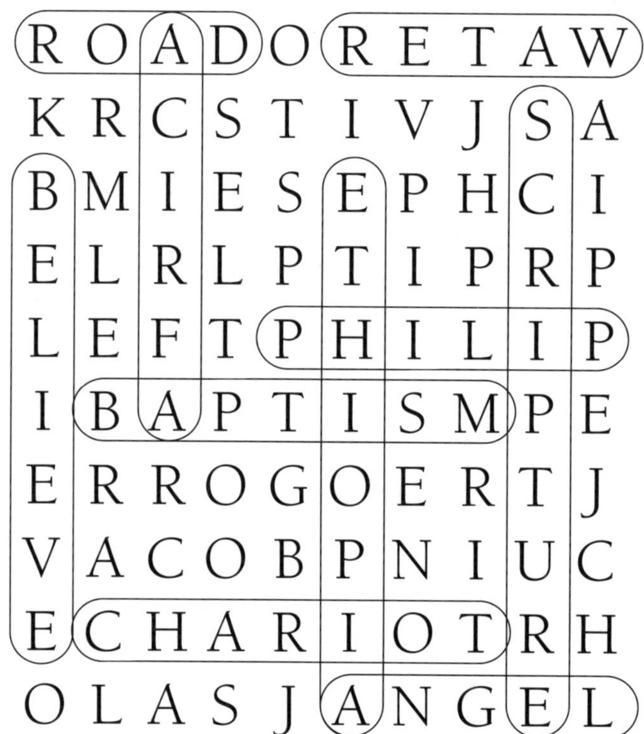

A Short but Rich Life (page 17)

¹B	A	P	T	I	Z	E	²D		³N	Y
L							R		N	
A			⁴J	A	C	Q	U	E	⁵S	
⁶C	A	M	E			M		O		
K			⁷S	C	A	⁸R	S		C	
R			U			U			I	
O			I		⁹U	N	C	L	E	
B		¹⁰A	T						T	
E							¹¹E	Y	¹²E	
¹³S	¹⁴M	A	L	L	¹⁵P	O	X		G	
	O				E				G	
	¹⁶M	O	H	A	W	K			S	

What Do You Mean Mass Is a Party? (page 23)

D, E, B, H, I, C, F, A, G

Who We Are, Whose We Are (page 27)

I am God's child

A Message From Paul (page 33)

8, 1, 4, 7, 2, 3, 6, 5

Figuring Out the Good News (page 43)

Faith without works is dead.